Sherlock Holmes and the Red Circle

Sir Arthur **Conan Doyle**

Illustrated by **Gianluca Garofalo**

Retold by **Gina D. B. Clemen**

Editor: Victoria Bradshaw
Design and art direction: Nadia Maestri
Computer graphics: Tiziana Pesce
Picture research: Laura Lagomarsino

© 2009 Black Cat

First edition: February 2009

DEALINK, DEAFLIX are trademarks licensed by De Agostini SpA

Picture credits:
By courtesy of the National Portrait Gallery, London: 4, 27 top; Album: 6; Mary
Evans Picture Library: 27 centre, 56, 57, 58; Library of Congress Prints and
Photographs Division, Washington, DC: 27 bottom, 67; © Bettman / Corbis: 28
top, 68; The Scottish National Portrait Gallery, Edinburgh: 28 centre; De
Agostini Picture Library: 28 bottom.

We would be happy to receive your comments and suggestions, and give
you any other information concerning our material.
info@blackcat-cideb.com
blackcat-cideb.com

Printed in Italy by Litoprint, Genova

Contents

The text is recorded in full.

 These symbols indicate the beginning and end of the passages linked to the listening activities.

Sir Arthur Conan Doyle (1927) by Henry L. Gates.

Sir Arthur Conan Doyle

track 02

Sir Arthur Conan Doyle was born in Edinburgh, Scotland, on 22 May 1859. When he was a young boy he liked reading books.

In 1876 he began studying medicine at Edinburgh University. One of his professors was Dr Joseph Bell. Dr Bell watched his patients closely so that he could understand their illness. Later Dr Bell became Conan Doyle's model for Sherlock Holmes.

In 1882 Conan Doyle became a doctor. He did not have many patients so he began writing his first Sherlock Holmes story, *A Study in Scarlet* (1887). The story was a big success.

In 1891 he wrote Sherlock Holmes stories for a monthly magazine called *The Strand*. Soon the clever detective and his friend Dr Watson became very popular in Great Britain. When Conan Doyle stopped writing Sherlock Holmes stories his readers got angry.

Finally in 1901 he started writing another Sherlock Holmes adventure called *The Hound of the Baskervilles*. A lot of other stories followed. His readers were very pleased and he continued writing about the famous detective until 1927.

Some famous Sherlock Holmes books are *The Sign of Four* (1890), *The Adventures of Sherlock Holmes* (1892), *The Return of Sherlock Holmes* (1905), *The Valley of Fear* (1915) and *The Case-Book of Sherlock Holmes* (1927). 'The Red Circle' is part of the book *His Last Bow* (1917).

Conan Doyle died in England on 7 July 1930.

1 COMPREHENSION CHECK
Are these sentences true (T) or false (F)? Correct the false ones.

		T	F
1	Sir Arthur Conan Doyle went to Edinburgh University because he wanted to become a doctor.	☐	☐
2	Dr Joseph Bell did not care about his patients.	☐	☐
3	The character Sherlock Holmes is a lot like Dr Joseph Bell.	☐	☐
4	Conan Doyle started writing his first Sherlock Holmes story because he needed money.	☐	☐
5	Conan Doyle stopped writing Sherlock Holmes stories because his readers were not interested in them.	☐	☐
6	He wrote *The Hound of the Baskervilles* in 1901.	☐	☐

Sherlock Holmes and Dr Watson

The story you are going to read takes place in London at the start of the twentieth century. It is about London's famous fictional detective, Sherlock Holmes and his good friend, Dr Watson. Dr Watson helps Holmes with his detective cases.

When Sherlock Holmes moved to London in 1874 he did not have much money and his family had to help him. In 1881 he decided to share the cost of his rooms at 221B Baker Street with Dr John H. Watson, and this is how Holmes and Watson became good friends.

André Morell as Dr Watson and Peter Cushing as Sherlock Holmes in the film *The Hound of the Baskervilles* (1959).

Watson tells us a lot of things about Holmes: he is not a difficult person to live with because he is quiet and has regular habits. For example, he usually goes to bed around ten at night and gets up very early in the morning. He works on his cases with a lot of energy, but sometimes he gets very bored and sits in the living room and does nothing.

Watson also tells us that he is untidy and his desk is always full of papers. Mrs Hudson is the housekeeper [1] who tidies the rooms. We know that Holmes plays the violin and wears Persian slippers [2] at home. He often uses chemistry equipment [3] to help him solve cases.

Holmes is an excellent detective and he often surprises Watson with his solutions to difficult cases.

PROJECT ON THE WEB

Let's visit the Sherlock Holmes Museum

Connect to the Internet and go to www.blackcat-cideb.com or www.cideb.it. Insert the title or part of the title of the book into our search engine.

Click on the Internet project link. Go down the page until you see this title and click on the relevant link for this project.

In London there is an interesting museum all about Sir Arthur Conan Doyle's famous detective. Find the answers to these questions on the site.

1 Where is the Sherlock Holmes Museum?
2 When did Sherlock Holmes live there, according to Sir Arthur Conan Doyle's stories?
3 When was the house built?
4 Where was Holmes's study?
5 What are some of things you can see in Holmes's study?

1. **housekeeper** : someone who does all the work in another person's house.

2. **Persian slippers** :

3. **chemistry equipment** :

The Characters

Sherlock Holmes

Dr Watson

Mrs Warren

Emilia Lucca

Gregson

Leverton

BEFORE YOU READ

track 04

1 LISTENING

Listen to the first part of Chapter One and choose the best answer – A, B or C.

1 Where is Sherlock Holmes?

A ☐ in one of Mrs Warren's rooms

B ☐ in Mrs Warren's study

C ☐ sitting at his desk

2 Mrs Warren has a problem with

A ☐ her new lodger.

B ☐ her old lodger.

C ☐ the cleaning girl.

3 What does Mrs Warren hear from the room?

A ☐ someone walking

B ☐ voices

C ☐ strange noises

4 The lodger came to Mrs Warren's house

A ☐ a week ago.

B ☐ ten days ago.

C ☐ two weeks ago.

5 Where are the lodger's two rooms?

A ☐ on the ground floor

B ☐ on the first floor

C ☐ at the top of the house

6 How much money did Mrs Warren ask the lodger for?

A ☐ two pounds a week

B ☐ five pounds a week

C ☐ ten pounds a week

7 Mrs Warren thought the lodger's first condition

A ☐ was not possible.

B ☐ was strange.

C ☐ was normal.

CHAPTER ONE

Mrs Warren's Problem

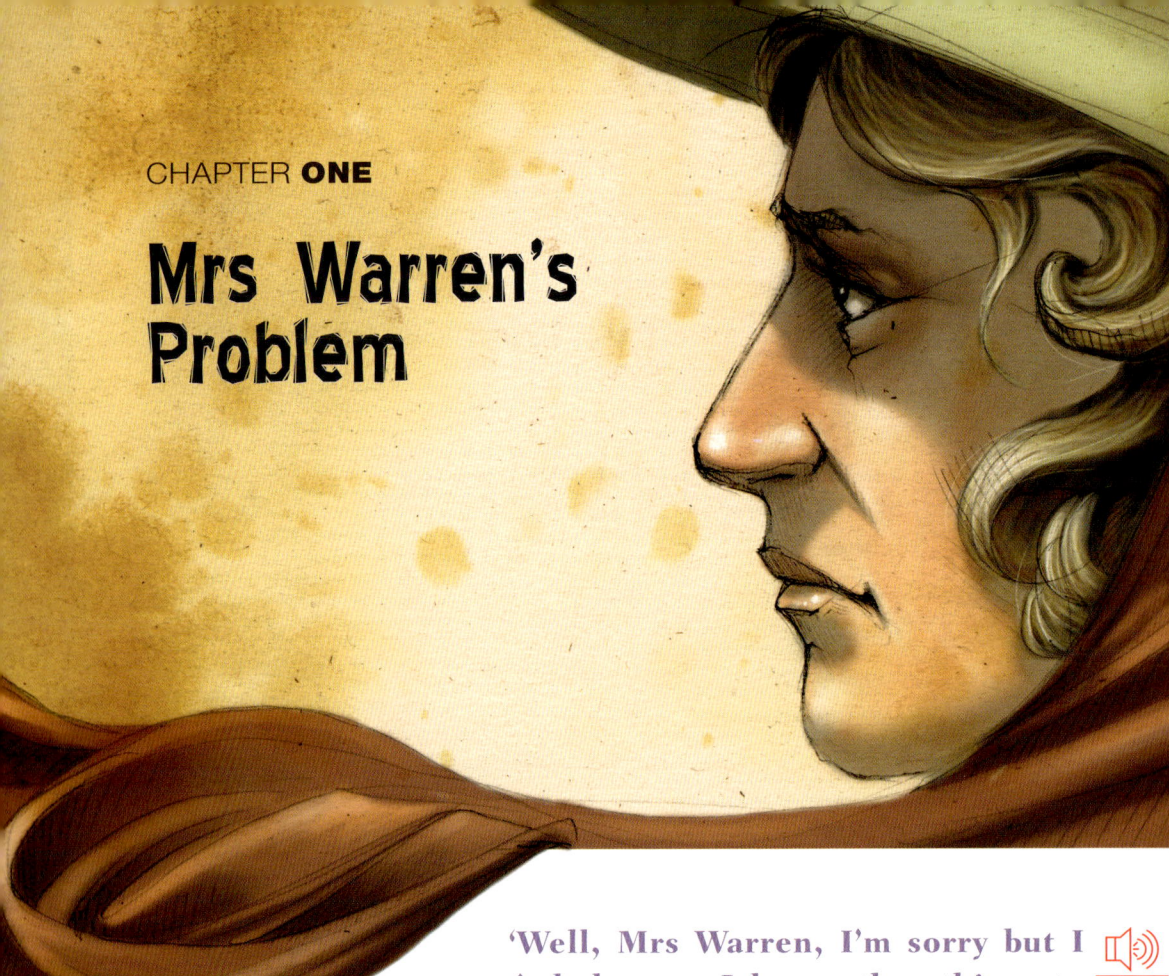

'Well, Mrs Warren, I'm sorry but I can't help you. I have other things to do,' said Sherlock Holmes, looking at the papers on his desk.

But Mrs Warren did not go away.

'You helped my lodger [1] Mr Hobbs last year,' said Mrs Warren, looking at Holmes.

'Yes, I remember,' said Holmes.

'Mr Hobbs said you are a kind, helpful man. Why can't you help me?' asked Mrs Warren.

Holmes looked at her and said, 'Alright, Mrs Warren, tell me about your problem. I understand your new lodger always stays in his rooms and you never see him. There's nothing strange about that!'

---

1. **lodger** : a person who rents a room in another person's house.

'But I'm really afraid and I can't sleep,' said Mrs Warren. 'I hear his quick footsteps from morning to night, but I never see him. Why is he hiding? My husband is worried too, but he is away all day at work. I'm alone at home with the girl who helps me clean, and I'm very frightened.'

Holmes looked at her kindly and said, 'Please sit down, Mrs Warren. Now if I decide to help you, I must know everything. Do you understand? The smallest thing can be the most important. You said that the man came ten days ago and paid you for two weeks. Is that correct?'

'Yes,' said Mrs Warren, 'I asked him to pay two pounds a week for a small sitting-room and a bedroom at the top of the house.'

'Well?' asked Holmes.

'He said, "I'll pay you five pounds a week if I can have the rooms on my conditions." [2]

I'm a poor woman, sir, and Mr Warren doesn't make much money. I needed the extra money. The man gave me ten pounds and said, "I can give you ten pounds every two weeks for a long time on my conditions."'

'What were his conditions?' asked Holmes.

'Well, he wanted a key to the house and that was alright. Lodgers often want a key. And he did not want anyone to disturb [3] him.'

'There is nothing strange about that, Mrs Warren,' said Holmes.

'No, but I never see him – no one sees him! He only went out of the house on the first night.'

---

2. **on my conditions** : following the rules I give you.
3. **disturb** : (here) go into his rooms.

'Oh, he went out on the first night?' asked Holmes.

'Yes, sir, and he came back very late when we were all in bed,' said Mrs Warren.

'But, his meals?' asked Holmes.

'Oh, we leave his meals on a chair outside his room when he rings the bell,' said Mrs Warren. 'And he rings again when he finishes eating. If he wants anything, he writes it in capital letters on a piece of paper and leaves it on the chair.'

'He writes in capital letters?' asked Holmes.

'Yes, sir, just the word in pencil, and nothing more,' said Mrs Warren. 'Look, here are the notes he writes. This one says SOAP. Here's another one that says MATCH. [4] And this is one he wrote this morning – it says DAILY GAZETTE. I leave the newspaper with his breakfast every morning.'

Mrs Warren gave Holmes the two pieces of paper and he looked at them with interest.

'Oh dear, Watson,' said Holmes, 'this is really a bit strange. Why does this man write in capital letters? It is much easier and quicker to write normally. What do you think, Watson?'

'He probably doesn't want Mrs Warren to see his handwriting,' I said.

'But why?' asked Holmes. 'Perhaps you're right, Watson. But why are his messages so short? Why doesn't he write in sentences?'

'I really don't know,' I said.

4. **match** :

UNDERSTANDING THE TEXT

KET

1 COMPREHENSION CHECK

Are these sentences 'Right' (A) or 'Wrong' (B)? If there is not enough information to answer 'Right' (A) or 'Wrong' (B), choose 'Doesn't say' (C). There is an example at the beginning (0).

0 There were lots of important papers on Sherlock Holmes's desk.

  A Right   B Wrong   C Doesn't say

1 In the past Mr Hobbs was Mrs Warren's lodger.

  A Right   B Wrong   C Doesn't say

2 Mrs Warren was a short, old woman.

  A Right   B Wrong   C Doesn't say

3 Sherlock Holmes decided to listen to Mrs Warren's problem.

  A Right   B Wrong   C Doesn't say

4 Mrs Warren and her husband were rich people.

  A Right   B Wrong   C Doesn't say

5 The lodger wanted a key to the house.

  A Right   B Wrong   C Doesn't say

6 The lodger had his meals in Mrs Warren's kitchen.

  A Right   B Wrong   C Doesn't say

7 He used a pencil to write his messages.

  A Right   B Wrong   C Doesn't say

8 Dr Watson was an old friend of Mrs Warren.

  A Right   B Wrong   C Doesn't say

2 PREPOSITIONS

Complete the sentences with a preposition from the box.

| about | at | behind | for | in | on | with |

1 The lodger wrote only one word ………… a piece of paper.

2 He always stayed ………… his rooms and never went out.

3 Holmes looked at the pieces of paper ………… interest.

4 Mrs Warren told Holmes and Watson ………… the strange lodger.

5 The bedroom was ………… the top of the house.

6 Mrs Warren talked to Holmes ………… two hours.

7 Holmes sat in a big chair ………… his desk.

3 MRS WARREN'S HOUSE

Mr and Mrs Warren live in a typical Victorian house like the one below. Look at the illustration of Mrs Warren's house and label each room with the words below. Use your dictionary to help you check any words you don't understand.

1	☐ dining room		7	☐ master bedroom
2	☐ kitchen		8	☐ pantry
3	☐ lodger's bathroom		9	☐ scullery
4	☐ lodger's bedroom		10	☐ servant's bedroom
5	☐ main entrance		11	☐ sitting-room
6	☐ master bathroom		12	☐ study

BEFORE YOU READ

1 **LISTENING**

track 05

Listen to the first part of Chapter Two and then choose the correct answer – A, B or C.

1 Mrs Warren's lodger was
- **A** ☐ over 30.
- **B** ☐ under 30.
- **C** ☐ under 20.

2 The lodger
- **A** ☐ came from another country.
- **B** ☐ did not speak English.
- **C** ☐ spoke bad English.

3 He wore
- **A** ☐ old clothes.
- **B** ☐ summer clothes.
- **C** ☐ dark colours.

4 Mrs Warren had an envelope
- **A** ☐ on the table.
- **B** ☐ in her pocket.
- **C** ☐ in her bag.

5 The lodger
- **A** ☐ was very hungry.
- **B** ☐ was not very hungry.
- **C** ☐ did not like Mrs Warren's meals.

2 **VOCABULARY**

Match the words to the pictures.

A luggage   **B** tray   **C** beard

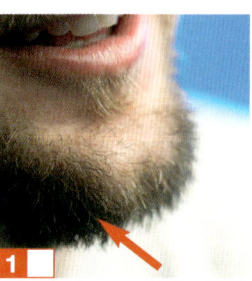

1 ☐

2 ☐

3 ☐

CHAPTER TWO

Secret Messages

Holmes looked at the two pieces of paper carefully. `track 05`

'This is interesting,' he said. 'He writes the words with a violet-coloured pencil. Mrs Warren, you said that the man is not tall or short and has dark hair and a beard. How old is he?'

'He's young, sir; not over thirty,' said Mrs Warren.

'Can you tell me something more about him?' asked Holmes.

'He spoke good English, but I'm sure he's a foreigner,' said Mrs Warren.

'Was he well-dressed?' asked Holmes.

'Yes, he was very well dressed in dark clothes,' answered Mrs Warren.

'Did he tell you his name?' asked Holmes.

'No, sir,' answered Mrs Warren.

'Does he receive any letters or friends?' asked Holmes.

'No, sir,' answered Mrs Warren.

'Do you or the girl go into his room to clean it?' asked Holmes.

'No, sir, he does it,' said Mrs Warren.

'Goodness!' said Holmes. 'That is surprising. Did he have any luggage?'

'He only had one big brown bag with him,' said Mrs Warren.

'We have to know more about him,' said Holmes. 'Did anything come out of that room?'

Mrs Warren took an envelope out of her bag and put it on the table. Inside the envelope there were two burnt matches and a cigarette stub. [1]

'They were on his tray this morning,' she said. 'I know that small things are important to you, Mr Holmes.'

---

1. **cigarette stub** : the end of a cigarette which people don't smoke.

Holmes picked them up and examined them.

'The matches aren't important. I think: 'he used them to light cigarettes. But, this cigarette stub is very strange. You said the man has a beard.'

'Yes, he does,' said Mrs Warren.

'I don't understand,' said Holmes. 'How can a man with a beard smoke a cigarette in that way? He will burn his beard! The cigarette stub is too short. Perhaps there are two people in the room, Mrs Warren.'

'Oh, no, he eats very little – not even enough for one person,' said Mrs Warren.

'At this point I think we must wait for a few more facts,' said Holmes. 'After all, he paid the rent and he does not cause trouble. If he wants to hide, it is not your business, Mrs Warren. We can't disturb him until there is a good reason. Now I have a good picture of your problem. Please tell me if anything new happens.'

'Thank you, Mr Holmes and Dr Watson,' said Mrs Warren leaving the room.

'Well, Watson, there are certainly some interesting things in this case,' said Holmes. 'I think the person in the rooms is probably not the one who rented them.'

'Why?' I asked surprised.

'Well, first of all there is the cigarette stub,' said Holmes. 'And then the lodger went out only once after he rented the rooms. He came back – or someone came back – when everyone in the house was sleeping. Was the person who went out the same person who came back late at night? We don't know. The man who rented the rooms spoke English well; but the other person wrote "match" and not "matches". This person probably does not know English well and that is why he writes short notes. Yes, Watson, I think the person in the rooms is not the same person who rented them.'

'How strange!' I said.

"Well, there is one thing we can do to find out more,' said Holmes. 'The person in Mrs Warren's rooms is alone and does not receive any letters or friends. How can he receive any news or messages from outside? Only by an advertisement [2] in a newspaper. There is no other way, and we even know the newspaper – the *Daily Gazette*.'

Holmes opened a big book where he put the personal advertisement sections of the London newspapers.

'Here are the *Daily Gazette* personal advertisements of the last two weeks. Hmm… "Lady with blue hat at Piccadilly Circus", "Jimmy, don't break your mother's heart". These don't interest me. Ah! Listen to this: "I will find a way to send you messages. For now, this column. G." Look at the date of the newspaper – it's two days after Mrs Warren's lodger rented the rooms. This mysterious person understands English even if he cannot write it.'

'Perhaps we can find more,' said Holmes. 'Yes, look, three days later. "Take care! The clouds will pass. G." There is nothing for another week and then another message, "If I send a message, remember the secret code: one A, two B and so on. You will hear from me soon. G." That was yesterday's paper and there is nothing in today's. It could be the lodger. Let's wait a bit, Watson. We'll know more soon.'

2. **advertisement** (here) : a personal message you put in the newspaper.

UNDERSTANDING THE TEXT

1 COMPREHENSION CHECK

The statements below are all incorrect. Rewrite them correctly.

1 Holmes thought the matches were very strange because the man had a beard.

   ....

2 Both Mrs Warren and Holmes thought there could be two people in the room.

   ....

3 Holmes thought that the person received messages in the post.

   ....

4 Holmes thought that the person in the rooms could not speak any English.

   ....

5 Holmes thought the name of the message sender began with the letter J.

   ....

6 Holmes found the last message in today's paper.

   ....

2 ODD ONE OUT

A Circle the word that doesn't belong and explain why.

1	ears	nose	eyes	beard
2	breakfast	meal	lunch	dinner
3	month	daily	week	year
4	London	England	France	Spain
5	bedroom	house	sitting-room	kitchen

B Now complete the sentences with the odd words.

A Mrs Warren had a big .... with a lot of rooms.

B The lodger had a dark ....

C Holmes and Watson lived in ....

D The lodger had a small .... in his room.

E She read the .... newspaper every evening.

3 **A SECRET MESSAGE**

The lodger receives the secret message below. What does it say? Work in pairs to solve it. Each letter (A-Z) is represented by a number (1-26). For example, A=24. This means that every time you see the number 24 in the message, you write 'A' under it. Use the letters already given and the numbers in the spaces to help you complete it.

24						–	22		–	–
A	**B**	**C**	**D**	**E**	**F**	**G**	**H**	**I**	**J**	**K**

16	–			–	–	10
L	**M**	**N**	**O**	**P**	**Q**	**R**

23	8		2	–	–		–
S	**T**	**U**	**V**	**W**	**X**	**Y**	**Z**

21	17		26	24	10	17	3	6	16		21	17	26	24	6	23	17
				A	R				L					A		S	

8	22	17	10	17		7	23		24		2	17	10	13
T	H		R				S		A		V		R	

26	16	17	2	17	10		16	5	25	14	5	25
	L		V		R		L					

14	17	8	17	26	8	7	2	17		22	17	10	17
		T			T		V			H		R	

Now in pairs write your own secret message. Once finished give it to another pair to solve. Give at least five letters to help them start. Use the spaces below to complete the key to the code.

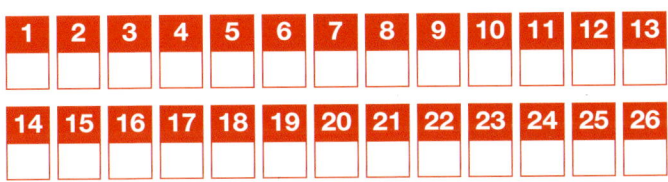

1	2	3	4	5	6	7	8	9	10	11	12	13

14	15	16	17	18	19	20	21	22	23	24	25	26

4 NOTICES

Which notice (A-H) says this (1-5)? There is an example at the beginning (0).

A Trains for
LONDON
Platform 6

B Sherlock Holmes
Detective
Appointments –
Wednesday and Friday
mornings only

C FLATS TO RENT
2 and 3 bedrooms only
Information next door

D Mrs Warren's
Lodging House

No animals allowed

E Sir William's
Bookshop
Books in many
languages
CLOSED ON SUNDAYS

F London Post Office
Telegram Service
OPEN ALL YEAR

G Brown's Luggage
Shop
Spring sale this week
Everything half price!

H Royal Theatre
Box Office
Open weekdays
only
10 a.m. to 2 p.m.

0	A.	You cannot catch a train for London on Platform 5.
1	.....	Things here cost less at the moment.
2	.....	You can buy a dictionary here.
3	.....	He can't see people in the afternoon.
4	.....	You can't keep a pet here.
5	.....	You can buy a ticket at lunch time on Tuesday.

5 'I THINK THE PERSON IN THE ROOMS IS NOT THE SAME PERSON WHO RENTED THEM'

5 **'I THINK THE PERSON IN THE ROOMS IS NOT THE SAME PERSON WHO RENTED THEM'**

Are you a good detective? What do you already know about the lodger? Discuss in class and make some notes.

- ....
- ....
- ....

- ....
- ....
- ....

Who do you think the lodger is? Discuss as a class.

- a dangerous criminal
- a woman
- a famous person

- a child
- a young man in danger
- someone else ...

T: GRADE 3

6 **SPEAKING: JOBS**

Holmes is a detective and Watson is a doctor. Talk about jobs you think are interesting. Use these questions to help you.

- What kind of job do you want to do in the future?
- Why do you want to do this job?
- What subjects do you need to study to do this job?
- Would you like to be a detective or a doctor? Why/Why not?

BEFORE YOU READ

track 07

1 **LISTENING**

Listen to the first part of Chapter Three. Are the following sentences true (T) or false (F)?

		T	F
1	Sherlock Holmes decided to go to Mrs Warren's house.	☐	☐
2	Mrs Warren wanted to call the police.	☐	☐
3	Mr Warren was at work.	☐	☐
4	The lodger was in danger.	☐	☐
5	Mrs Warren wanted to see the lodger.	☐	☐

Victorian Writers

Sir Arthur Conan Doyle started writing his stories about Sherlock Holmes in the late nineteenth century, during Victorian times. A lot of Britain's greatest writers wrote at this time and this inspired him.

During the nineteenth century educational possibilities were slowly getting better, and more and more people were learning to read and write. Without the radio, cinema or television, reading was the favourite type of entertainment. People loved reading novels, newspapers, magazines, academic [1] books and even comics.

In the 1850s the government started building public libraries in towns and cities all over Great Britain. Books were too expensive to buy for most people, but in these new libraries more people had the possibility to read a lot of different books.

The Daily Telegraph, started in 1855, became the first penny paper. [2] The paper was a big success, and quickly became the best-selling newspaper. Because of this, more and more people could read the newspaper every day.

The first children's comics with funny cartoons and adventures also came out in the 1850s and children had great fun reading them.

In Victorian times novels were sometimes published in chapters in magazines and newspapers. Every week or month people could read a new chapter of a story. This continued for months, and sometimes years, until the story was finished.

As a result of all these changes some authors became very popular. Here are some of them.

---

1. **academic** : something factual that you study.
2. **penny paper** : a newspaper that cost only one penny.

Charles Dickens (1812-70)

As a child Charles Dickens was poor. He left school at a young age to work in a factory for long hours. He never forgot this bad experience. His first novel was *The Pickwick Papers* (1837) and it was a success. He wrote fourteen important novels, including *Oliver Twist* (1839) and *David Copperfield* (1849-50). He wrote about the poor people and the social problems at that time.

Anna Sewell (1820-78)

In 1877 Anna Sewell wrote *Black Beauty*. It was about the life and adventures of a horse. After reading this book people began to understand that animals were living creatures and it was wrong to mistreat them.

Wilkie Collins (1824-89)

In 1868 Wilkie Collins published *The Moonstone* with one of the first detectives in English fiction, Sergeant Cuff. The novel became very popular and people started reading detective fiction.

Lewis Carroll (1832-98)

Lewis Carroll wrote the first fantasy story for children, called *Alice's Adventures in Wonderland* (1865). It was a best seller. Victorian children loved the book with its exciting adventures and beautiful illustrations by Sir John Tenniel.

Robert Louis Stevenson (1850-94)

In 1883 Robert Louis Stevenson wrote a great adventure book for young people called *Treasure Island*. It was about a young boy's adventures with pirates at sea. He also wrote other adventure stories, like *Kidnapped* (1886) and *The Black Arrow* (1888).

Rudyard Kipling (1865-1936)

Rudyard Kipling wrote *The Jungle Book* (1894), *The Second Jungle Book* (1895) and *Just So Stories* (1902); they were very popular with children. Most of the characters of these books were animals.

1 COMPREHENSION CHECK

Are the following sentences true (T) or false (F)? Correct the false ones.

T F

1 In the 19th century only rich people could read and write. ☐ ☐
2 After the 1850s there were more public libraries
   in Great Britain. ☐ ☐
3 Charles Dickens wrote only about rich people. ☐ ☐
4 Wilkie Collins wrote stories for children. ☐ ☐
5 Robert Louis Stevenson wrote *The Jungle Book* in 1894. ☐ ☐

PROJECT ON THE WEB

Let's find out more about these Victorian writers

Connect to the Internet and go to www.blackcat-cideb.com or
www.cideb.it. Insert the title or part of the title of the book into our
search engine.

Click on the Internet project link. Go down the page until you see this
title and click on the relevant link for this project.

Choose one of the authors above, or another from the late 19th to early
20th centuries and find out more about their lives and the books they
wrote. Prepare a report for the class.

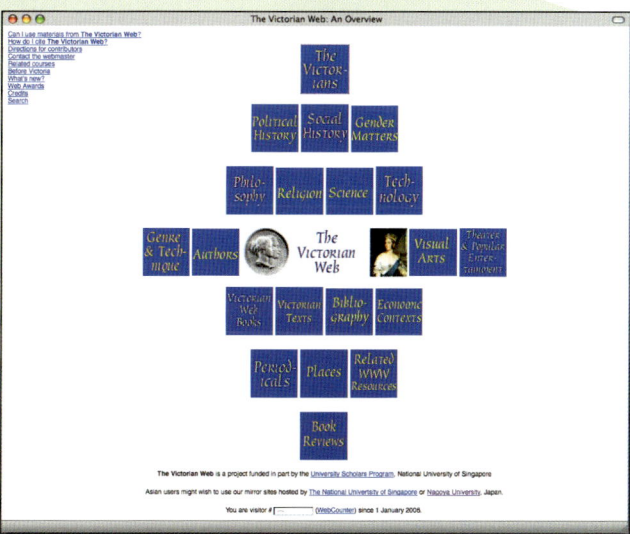

CHAPTER THREE

The Face in the Mirror

The next morning Holmes was sitting at his desk with a big smile on his face.

track 07

'Listen to this, Watson,' he said reading the newspaper aloud. [1] 'Tall red house with white windows; third floor; second window on left; after dark. G" This is a clear message. After breakfast we'll go and visit Mrs Warren's house.'

'Good idea!' I said.

We got to Mrs Warren's house and we waited for her in the sitting-room. She suddenly ran into the room and said angrily, 'I must call the police, Mr Holmes, but I wanted to talk to you first. That man must leave this house! Something terrible happened to my husband this morning!'

'What happened to Mr Warren?' asked Holmes.

'This morning he went to work before seven o'clock. He walked down the road a few steps and suddenly two men came up behind

---

1. **aloud** : using his voice so others can hear him.

him. They threw a coat over his head and pushed him into a cab. [2] They drove around for an hour and then opened the door and pushed him out on Hampstead Heath. [3] When he got home the poor man was very frightened and now he's sleeping upstairs.'

'Very interesting,' said Holmes. 'Did he see the men? Did he hear them speak?'

'No, he didn't,' said Mrs Warren, 'but he thinks there were two or three men.'

'And do you think this has something to do with your lodger?' asked Holmes.

'Of course!' said Mrs Warren. 'My husband never had such a problem before. I don't want that lodger in this house. Money isn't everything!'

'Wait a moment, please,' said Holmes. 'I think your lodger is in some kind of danger. Those men were probably waiting for him outside your door this morning. They thought your husband was the lodger because it was still dark at that time. When they discovered it was the wrong man, they let your husband go.'

'What must I do?' asked Mrs Warren.

'I want to see your lodger,' said Holmes.

'But how can you see him?' asked Mrs Warren. 'No one can see him.'

end

'He has to open the door and take the tray with his meal into his room. Watson and I can hide and watch him do it.'

Mrs Warren thought for a moment and said, 'Yes, you can! There's a small cupboard near his room and I can put up a mirror,

2. **cab** :
3. **Hampstead Heath** : a large park in north London.

and if you are behind the door...'

'Excellent idea!' said Holmes. 'When does he eat lunch?'

'At about one o'clock.'

'Good,' said Holmes. 'Dr Watson and I will come to your house before one o'clock. Goodbye, Mrs Warren.'

At half past twelve we were outside Mrs Warren's house. Holmes pointed to one of the houses in opposite.

'Look, Watson!' he said. '"Tall red house with white windows". That's the house in the newspaper message. Now we know the place and the secret code – our job is easy! Look, there's a 'To Rent' sign in the window. It must be an empty flat.'

'Yes, I'm sure it is,' I said looking at the red house.

Holmes rang the bell of Mrs Warren's house and she opened the door.

'I have everything ready for you,' she said. 'Please come up and I'll show you the cupboard.'

'Thank you, Mrs Warren,' said Holmes.

Holmes and I followed Mrs Warren upstairs quietly. The cupboard was a very good place to hide. Mrs Warren put the mirror in a position so that we could see the door of the lodger's rooms. We sat down and waited. Then we heard the lodger ring for lunch and Mrs Warren came up with the tray. She put it down on a chair near the closed door and left. We heard her heavy footsteps going down the stairs and we kept our eyes on the mirror.

'When is the lodger going to open the door?' I whispered. [4]

'Probably very soon,' Holmes whispered back.

4. **whispered** : said very quietly.

Suddenly we heard the sound of a key opening the door. Two thin hands came out quickly and took the tray from the chair. But a moment later the hands put back the tray. I saw a beautiful but frightened face, looking at the open door of the cupboard. Then

the lodger's door closed quickly and the key turned. Everything was silent again and we went back downstairs.

'I will come back again this evening,' said Holmes to Mrs Warren. 'I think we can discuss this better at Baker Street, Watson.'

UNDERSTANDING THE TEXT

KET

1 COMPREHENSION CHECK

Read these sentences about Chapter Three. Choose the correct answer (A, B or C). There is an example at the beginning (0).

0 Holmes was sitting at his desk
- A ☐ writing a letter.
- B ☑ reading the newspaper.
- C ☐ having breakfast.

1 Mrs Warren was angry
- A ☐ at Sherlock Holmes and Dr Watson.
- B ☐ because something happened to her husband.
- C ☐ at the police.

2 Someone pushed Mr Warren
- A ☐ into a cab.
- B ☐ out of a cab.
- C ☐ in front of a cab.

3 Sherlock Holmes thought the lodger
- A ☐ went to work before seven o'clock.
- B ☐ threw a coat over Mr Warren's head.
- C ☐ was in danger.

4 The lodger always had lunch
- A ☐ at one o'clock.
- B ☐ after one o'clock.
- C ☐ before one o'clock.

5 The tall red house with white windows was
- A ☐ next to Mrs Warren's house.
- B ☐ behind Mrs Warren's house.
- C ☐ in front of Mrs Warren's house.

6 Holmes and Watson hid in a cupboard because
- A ☐ they were afraid of the lodger.
- B ☐ Mrs Warren was looking for them.
- C ☐ they wanted to see the lodger.

HOLMES AND I FOLLOWED MRS WARREN UPSTAIRS

We form the past simple of regular verbs by adding **-ed** to the verb.

I/you/he/she/it/we/you/they   *talked, called, worked*

Some verbs end in a consonant + -y. We change the -y to **i** and add **-ed**.

carry – carried   study – studied   hurry – hurried

But if verbs end in a vowel + -y, the -y does not change.

play – played   enjoy – enjoyed   stay – stayed

2 THE PAST SIMPLE – REGULAR VERBS
Complete the sentences with the past simple form of a verb from the box.

listen   look   open   stayed   study   visit   wait

1 The lodger .... the door quickly and took the tray.
2 Holmes and Watson .... the house at one o'clock.
3 Watson .... to Holmes read the newspaper.
4 Holmes .... the contents of the envelope carefully.
5 Holmes and Watson .... at the building opposite Mrs Warren's house.
6 Holmes and Watson .... inside the cupboard and .... for the lodger to open the door.

3 OPPOSITES
Match a word from the first column to one from the second column to make opposites.

1 ☐ push
2 ☐ wrong
3 ☐ near
4 ☐ easy
5 ☐ dark
6 ☐ beautiful
7 ☐ quickly
8 ☐ silent

A slowly
B light
C pull
D noisy
E right
F difficult
G far
H ugly

Now write some sentences using some of the opposites above.

....
....

BEFORE YOU READ

1 LISTENING

Listen to the first part of Chapter Four and choose the correct answer – A, B or C.

track 08

1 The man cannot visit the woman because
   A ☐ he doesn't want to see her.
   B ☐ he is trying to protect her.
   C ☐ he is her enemy.

2 The weather in the evening was
   A ☐ warm.
   B ☐ wet.
   C ☐ cold.

3 What could Holmes and Watson see from Mrs Warren's sitting-room?
   A ☐ the tall red building
   B ☐ the lodger's door
   C ☐ a light in the lodger's window

4 What does the dark figure use to send the message?
   A ☐ a match
   B ☐ the flame of a candle
   C ☐ two candles

5 What does the first message say?
   A ☐ Go away!
   B ☐ Danger!
   C ☐ Be careful!

6 Who was standing at the door of the building?
   A ☐ a man in a dark coat
   B ☐ the lodger
   C ☐ the beautiful young woman

CHAPTER **FOUR**

Danger!

'I was right, Watson,' said Holmes, sitting in his big armchair. 'The lodger we just saw is not the man Mrs Warren knows; it's a beautiful young woman!'

'Yes,' I said, 'and she saw us.'

'Well, she saw something that frightened her,' said Holmes. 'Everything is a little clearer now, isn't it? A man and a woman come to London to get away from a dangerous situation. The man has some work that he must do and leaves the woman in a safe place. This was not easy, but he had a clever plan and he hid her well. Not even Mrs Warren knows who the lodger is! She writes in capital letters because she has a woman's handwriting. She didn't want anyone to know about her. The man cannot come near the woman because their enemies [1] could find her; so he writes messages in the newspapers. So far everything is clear.'

'But what is behind this?' I asked.

---

1. **enemies** : people who are not your friends.

'Ah, yes,' Watson,' said Holmes, 'what is behind this? Mrs Warren's problem is bigger than I thought. We saw the young woman's frightened face and we heard what happened to Mr Warren. This is a matter of life and death, dear Watson. But the enemy does not know about the change of lodger. It is all very strange.'

It was a cold winter evening when we went back to Mrs Warren's house. We decided to sit in her dark sitting-room in front of the big window. From there we could see a light on the third floor of the red building.

'Someone is in that room,' said Holmes, moving closer to the window. 'I can see a dark figure. There he is again! He has a candle in his hand and he is looking out of the window. Now he is starting to send a message with the flame of the candle. [2] Let's both try and read the message, Watson. One flash – that's an "A". Now, how many flashes did he make? Twenty. Is that right, Watson?'

'Yes, he made twenty flashes,' I said.

'That means T. A, T... At – that's clear. Now another T. That's the beginning of a new word. Hmm...TENTA. He stopped. That can't be the message. AT, TENTA doesn't mean anything. Perhaps it's three words – AT, TEN, TA, or perhaps TA is part of the person's name. There it goes again! What's that? ATTE – it's the same message again. How strange, Watson! Now he is sending a third message – ATTENTA. He left the window. I think the message is finished. What do you think, Watson?'

'I don't know, Holmes,' I said.

Suddenly Holmes laughed and said, 'Why of course, the

2. **flame of the candle :**

message is in Italian! The A at the end of the word means that the message is for a woman. It means 'Be careful! Be careful! Be careful!' How's that, Watson?'

'I think you're right, Holmes,' I said.

'I'm certain!' said Holmes. 'But be careful of what? Wait! He's at the window again.'

We saw the dark figure of a man who started sending messages again. This time he sent the message very quickly and it was difficult to follow it.

'PERICOLO! What's that, Watson?' said Holmes. 'Isn't that danger in Italian? Yes, of course, it's a danger signal. Look, there he goes again! PERI...What happened?'

The light went away and the third floor of the building was dark. The message suddenly stopped. What happened? Holmes and I had the same thought. Holmes jumped up from his chair.

'Watson, this is serious,' he cried. 'Something terrible is happening. Why did the message stop? I want to call Scotland Yard [3] but we can't go away now.'

'What shall we do?' I asked.

'We need more facts,' said Holmes. 'Come on, Watson, let's go and see what's happening.'

Holmes and I walked quickly out of the house and across the street. I looked back at Mrs Warren's house. On the top floor I could see a woman's head at the window. She was waiting for the message to continue.

There was a man in a dark coat standing at the door of the red building. When he saw us he called, 'Holmes! Watson!'

'Gregson!' said Holmes, looking at the Scotland Yard detective. 'Why are you here?'

end

3. **Scotland Yard** : the London police.

'I'm here for the same reason you're here,' said Gregson. 'How did you find out about this?'

'In a different way from you,' said Holmes. 'I was looking at the signals.'

'What signals?' asked Gregson.

'The signals from the window,' said Holmes. 'They suddenly stopped and Watson and I came here to see why. But since the case is in your hands we can go.'

'Wait a moment!' cried Gregson. 'I always feel better with you with me. There is only one way out from these flats – the front door. So we have him!'

'Who is he?' asked Holmes.

'You don't know?' asked Gregson, surprised. 'Well, for once I know more than you, Mr Holmes.'

UNDERSTANDING THE TEXT

1 COMPREHENSION CHECK

Match each sentence (1–10) to its correct ending (A–J) to make a summary of Chapter Four.

1 ☐ The lodger in Mrs Warren's house
2 ☐ A man and woman came to London because
3 ☐ The man left the woman
4 ☐ He sent her messages
5 ☐ From Mrs Warren's sitting-room Holmes and Watson saw
6 ☐ The man in the room on the third floor
7 ☐ The messages were
8 ☐ The man told the woman
9 ☐ When the messages suddenly stopped
10 ☐ Holmes and Watson met

A through the newspaper.
B was sending messages with the flame of a candle.
C they were in danger.
D a policeman from Scotland Yard.
E a light on the third floor of the red building.
F in a safe place.
G to be careful.
H was a beautiful young woman.
I in another language.
J Holmes and Watson went to the red building.

2 QUESTION WORDS

Complete the questions (1–6) with the correct question word from the box. Then match each question to an answer (A–F).

When	How	Who	Where	What	Why

1 ☐ .... did Holmes meet outside the red building?
2 ☐ .... did Holmes and Watson go to Mrs Warren's house?
3 ☐ .... was the tall red building?
4 ☐ .... did the man send the messages?
5 ☐ .... was Holmes looking at?
6 ☐ .... did the man and woman go to London?

A He was looking at the signals from the window.

B They went in the evening.

C He met Gregson from Scotland Yard.

D He used a candle.

E Because they wanted to get away from danger.

F It was in front of Mrs Warren's house.

 KET

3 VOCABULARY

Read the descriptions of some words from Chapter Four. What is the word for each one? The first letter is already there. There is one space for each other letter in the word. There is an example at the beginning (0).

0	You read it every day.	N EWSPAPER
1	A type of comfortable seat.	A _ _ _ _ _ _ _
2	To be afraid of something.	F _ _ _ _ _ _ _ _
3	The opposite of safe.	D _ _ _ _ _ _ _
4	The opposite of a friend.	E _ _ _ _
5	It has a flame and it makes light.	C _ _ _ _ _

Now find the words in the word square.

```
B A O E T O R E N S
U R N C A N D L E I
E M E D W U M E W G
V C S N R O A N S U
T H I C E M E F P A
E A N K U M G J A U
P I U A W I Y O P T
F R I G H T E N E D
I L E T K O S R R H
S D A N G E R O U S
```

4 WRITING

Complete Gregson's diary. Write ONE word for each space.

This evening (**1**)...!.... had a big surprise – I saw London's most famous detective, Sherlock Holmes! He is (**2**)........ old friend but I rarely see (**3**)........ . He was (**4**)........ his friend Dr Watson. They (**5**)........ both at the red building on Howe Street.
I worked with Holmes and Watson last year (**6**)........ January. We (**7**)........ looking for a dangerous criminal called John Prince (**8**)........ week I am working on an important case. Perhaps Holmes can help me with (**9**)........ . He is a very clever man and a good friend.

 KET

5 CONVERSATION

Complete the conversation between Sherlock Holmes and Dr Watson. Write the correct letter next to the number. There is an example at the beginning (0).

0 **Holmes:** Do you want to go to the British Museum tomorrow?
   Watson: ...B.....

1 **Holmes:** What time can we meet?
   Watson: ....

2 **Holmes:** What exhibition do you want to see?
   Watson: ....

3 **Holmes:** Well, there's a great exhibition on Italian painters of the 1400s.
   Watson: ....

4 **Holmes:** And there's another wonderful exhibition on French painters of the 1800s.
   Watson: ....

5 **Holmes:** I thought you liked French painters.
   Watson: ....

A	Maybe not this time.	E	Early in the afternoon.
B	Yes, I'm free tomorrow.	F	No, I don't like it.
C	I do, but we'll probably be too tired.	G	You choose.
D	I like.	H	That sounds good.

BEFORE YOU READ

track 09

1 LISTENING

Listen to the first part of Chapter Five and choose the correct answer – A, B or C.

1 Where did Sherlock Holmes, Watson and Gregson meet?

A ☐ at Pinkerton's Detective Agency

B ☐ at Scotland Yard

C ☐ in the street

2 Who introduced Mr Leverton to Sherlock Holmes?

A ☐ Dr Watson

B ☐ Mr Gregson

C ☐ Giuseppe Gorgiano

3 Who did Mr Leverton work for?

A ☐ Scotland Yard

B ☐ Sherlock Holmes

C ☐ Pinkerton's Detective Agency

4 Who was Gorgiano?

A ☐ a terrible criminal

B ☐ an American detective

C ☐ a man who lived in the tall red building

5 What information did Holmes give the two detectives?

A ☐ information about the signals

B ☐ information about Mrs Warren's lodger

C ☐ information about Giuseppe Gorgiano

6 What does Leverton usually need to arrest a person?

A ☐ help from Sherlock Holmes

B ☐ an arrest warrant

C ☐ a message from the Red Circle

7 Who decides that they can go into the building?

A ☐ Sharlock Holmes

B ☐ Mr Leverton

C ☐ Mr Gregson

CHAPTER FIVE

Giuseppe Gorgiano

Holmes, Gregson and I were standing outside the tall red building. **Suddenly a tall man got out of a cab on the other side of the street and came to us.**

Mr Gregson turned to him and said, 'Mr Leverton, this is Sherlock Holmes.' Then he turned to Holmes and said, 'This is Mr Leverton of Pinkerton's Detective Agency [1] in America.'

'Sir, I am very pleased to meet you,' said Holmes. 'You're the hero of several important cases.'

The young American became embarrassed at the words of Holmes.

'I'm on the most important case of my life now,' said Leverton. 'If I can get Gorgiano…'

'What! Gorgiano of the Red Circle?" asked Holmes.

---

1. **Pinkerton's Detective Agency** : a famous American detective agency of the 19th century.

'Oh, is he known in Europe too?' said Leverton. 'Well, we know all about him in America. He's a terrible criminal who killed fifty people and I want to arrest him. I followed him from New York and I'm watching him carefully here in London. Mr Gregson and I followed him to this building. There is only one door here so he can't get away. Three men came out of this building after he went in. But he wasn't one of them.'

'Mr Holmes talked about signals,' said Gregson. 'I'm sure he knows more than we do.'

Holmes explained everything we knew to Gregson and Leverton.

'Gorgiano knows we're looking for him,' said the American detective.

'How do you know?' asked Holmes.

'Well, it seems that way, doesn't it?' said Leverton. 'This evening he sent messages to a member of the Red Circle. There are several members here in London and they know we're looking for them. What can we do, Mr Holmes?'

'We must go up at once and see,' said Holmes.

'But I can't arrest him,' said Leverton. 'I don't have an arrest warrant.'[2]

'That man is in an empty flat that is not his home,' said Gregson. 'That's a good reason to arrest him. Then perhaps the New York police can help us to keep him in prison.'

We went into the building and Leverton ran up the stairs first to arrest the killer. But Gregson wanted to be the first and pushed him back. After all, Gregson was part of the London police and we were in London.

2. **warrant** : a document that allows a policeman to arrest someone.

When we got to the third floor the door of the flat was partly open. Gregson pushed it open and we all walked in. Everything was dark and silent inside. I lit [3] the detective's lantern and suddenly we saw something terrible – a lot of blood on the floor.

3. **lit** : past tense of 'to light', to create light, here with a match.

There were red steps on the floor that came from a closed room. Gregson opened the door and held the lantern in front of him. We all looked inside the room.

On the floor of the empty room we saw a very big man with a circle of blood around his head. There was a big knife in his neck and another, bigger knife near his hand.

'It's Gorgiano!' cried the American detective loudly. 'Gorgiano! Someone got here before us!'

'Here is the candle at the window, Mr Holmes,' said Gregson. 'But, what are you doing?'

Holmes lit the candle and moved it across the window several times. Then he blew it out and put it down.

'I think this will help,' he said and walked over to the other two men.

'Mr Leverton, you said three people came out of the building,' said Holmes. 'Did you look at them?'

'Yes, I did,' said Leverton.

'Was there a man between twenty and thirty years old with dark hair and a beard?' asked Holmes.

'Yes, there was,' said Leverton.

'I think he is your man,' said Holmes. 'That is why I called his lady here.'

We all turned around when we heard this. And at the door there was a tall, beautiful woman – Mrs Warren's mysterious lodger.

She slowly walked into the room. Her face was white and her frightened eyes looked at the body of the huge [4] man on the floor.

4. **huge** : very big.

UNDERSTANDING THE TEXT

 KET

1 COMPREHENSION CHECK

Are these sentences 'Right' (A) or 'Wrong' (B)? If there is not enough information to answer 'Right' or 'Wrong' (B), choose 'Doesn't say' (C). There is an example at the beginning (0).

0 The tall man in the cab came from the United States of America.

Ⓐ Right   **B** Wrong   **C** Doesn't say

1 Leverton was new at Pinkerton's Detective Agency.

A Right   **B** Wrong   **C** Doesn't say

2 Gorgiano was part of a secret society called the Red Circle.

A Right   **B** Wrong   **C** Doesn't say

3 Gorgiano and two other men came out of the building.

A Right   **B** Wrong   **C** Doesn't say

4 Holmes did not tell Gregson and Leverton about the signals.

A Right   **B** Wrong   **C** Doesn't say

5 Leverton and Gregson ran up the stairs to the third floor.

A Right   **B** Wrong   **C** Doesn't say

6 There were two big knives in Gorgiano's body.

A Right   **B** Wrong   **C** Doesn't say

7 Holmes made signals at the window with a candle.

A Right   **B** Wrong   **C** Doesn't say

8 Mrs Warren's lodger came to the flat at midnight.

A Right   **B** Wrong   **C** Doesn't say

2 ADJECTIVES

Unscramble the adjectives in the box and use them to complete the sentences.

UTUELABFI   TAOMPITRN   DEHNFIREGT   REILEBTR

1 Gorgiano was a .... killer.
2 The young woman was tall and very ....
3 She was .... when she saw the body on the floor.
4 Leverton was an .... detective in New York City.

'IT'S GORGIANO!' CRIED THE AMERICAN DETECTIVE LOUDLY

Loudly is an adverb. We use adverbs with verbs to tell us **when**, **where** or **how** something happens.

We form most adverbs by adding -ly to the end of an adjective.

ADJECTIVE	ADVERB
slow	slowly
quiet	quietly

But when the adjective ends in a consonant + -y, we change the -y to -ily.

| easy | easily |
| happy | happily |

Be careful: the adverb of good is irregular

| good | well |

3 ADVERBS

Complete the sentences with the correct adverb from the box.

correct   angry   silent   slow   good   quick

1 Holmes and Watson were tired and walked up the stairs ....
2 'I'm going to call the police!' said Mrs Warren ....
3 Gregson ran out of the building ....
4 The lodger spoke English ....
5 Her English was bad and she could not spell the word ....
6 Mrs Warren closed the door .... because her husband was sleeping.

KET

4 LISTENING

Listen to the conversation between Gregson and Leverton. For each question choose the correct answer – A, B or C.

track 10

0 When did Leverton leave Boston?

31 December
A ☐

1 January
B ✓

2 January
C ☐

1 How did Gregson travel from New York to Liverpool?

 A
 B
 C

2 How long did it take Leverton to get across the Atlantic Ocean?

 A
 B
 C

3 How did Leverton get to San Francisco?

 A
 B
 C

4 Where are Leverton and Gregson going to meet?

 A
 B
 C

Police and Detectives in the 19th Century

track 11

In the early part of the nineteenth century there was a lot of crime in London. The city was crowded and criminals could hide easily. It was often not safe to walk down the dark streets.

In 1829 Sir Robert (Bobby) Peel (1788-1850) started the London Metropolitan Police at Scotland Yard. It was the world's first modern police force with around 1,000 men. The police wore uniforms and were known as 'peelers' or 'bobbies', both because of Robert Peel's name, the work of the police was to stop crime in the city streets.

At first the people of London did not like the police, but when there was less crime in the city, they started to understand that the police were important. After 1856 there were police forces all over Great Britain. The Metropolitan Police Force became a model for the New York City Police in 1850 and for other police forces around the world.

A row of uniformed Victorian policemen (about 1850).

A policeman on duty on a snowy night, illustration from *The Graphic* (1872).

In 1842 the first detective department was started at Scotland Yard. It had only two inspectors and six sergeants. Detectives did not wear uniforms and they investigated more complicated crimes. In 1878 the detective department became the 'Criminal Investigation Department' (CID). Mr Gregson in 'The Red Circle' worked for this department.

In 'The Red Circle' Mr Leverton worked for the Pinkerton Detective Agency in the United States. This agency was created by Allan Pinkerton in Chicago in 1850 and today it is the oldest in America. Allan Pinkerton became famous when he discovered a plan to kill president-elect [1] Abraham Lincoln. During the American Civil War President Lincoln used Pinkerton Detectives to protect himself and his family.

1. **president-elect** : at that time he was waiting to officially become the president after winning the election.

Sometimes detectives did not do a good job and made a lot of mistakes. Other times it took them months to solve a case. And at times they never solved the case. Some people paid a private detective (like the character of Sherlock Holmes) to solve difficult cases.

In Conan Doyle's stories Sherlock Holmes solved cases with modern scientific methods called forensic methods. He used chemical analysis, microscopes, fingerprints, photographs, studies of handwriting and footprints. In real life detectives did not use these methods yet. In 1901 Scotland Yard started using fingerprints to solve cases.

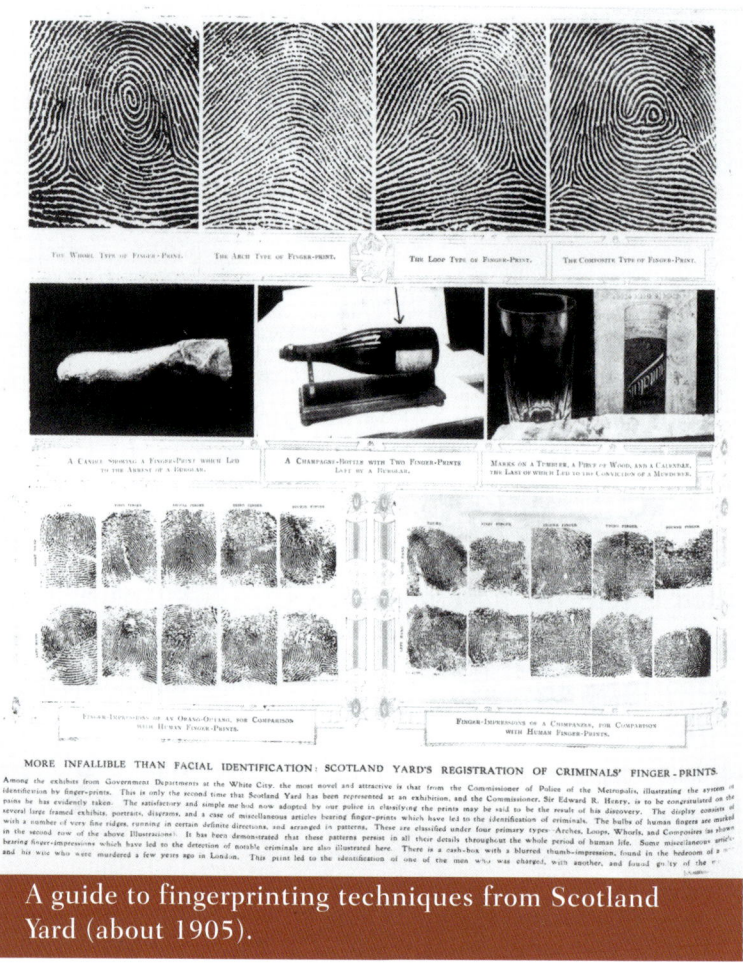

A guide to fingerprinting techniques from Scotland Yard (about 1905).

1 COMPREHENSION CHECK

Are the following sentences true (T) or false (F)? Correct the false ones.

		T	F
1	London was a dangerous city in the nineteenth century.	☐	☐
2	Sir Robert Peel started the London Metropolitan Police in Scotland.	☐	☐
3	The police were not popular at first.	☐	☐
4	There were only six men in the first detective department.	☐	☐
5	Forensic methods were used to solve cases before Conan Doyle wrote his Sherlock Holmes stories.	☐	☐

2 VOCABULARY – FORENSIC METHODS

Match the forensic methods or equipment in the box to each of the pictures.

chemical analysis   fingerprint matching   footprint matching
handwriting analysis   microscope   photograph analysis

1 _____

2 _____

3 _____

4 _____

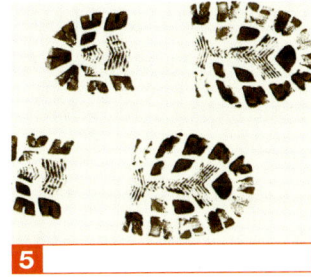

5 _____

6 _____

Emilia's Story

The beautiful young woman stood in the empty room and looked sadly at the body of the dead man. Then she looked at us with her dark eyes.

'But you! Are you the police?' she asked.

'Yes, we are the police,' said Gregson.

She looked around the dark room.

'But then, where is Gennaro?' she asked. 'Gennaro Lucca is my husband. I am Emilia Lucca and we come from New York. Where is Gennaro? He just called me from this window and I ran here.'

'I called you,' said Holmes.

'You! How could you call me?' asked Emilia Lucca.

'Your secret code was not difficult, madam,' said Holmes. 'We needed you here, so I flashed "vieni" [1] at the window.'

---

1. **vieni** : this word means 'come' in Italian.

The beautiful Italian woman looked at Holmes with surprise.

'I do not understand how you know these things,' she said. 'Giuseppe Gorgiano – how did he –' She stopped and then suddenly said, 'Now I understand! Gennaro killed this monster with his strong hands.'

'Well, Mrs Lucca,' said Gregson, putting his hand on her arm, 'I don't really know who you are or what you are. But you know a lot about this case. Please come to Scotland Yard with me.'

'One moment, Gregson,' said Holmes. 'I think this lady has several important things to tell us.'

Holmes turned to Mrs Lucca and said, 'Madam, your husband will be arrested for killing this man. What Gennaro did is very wrong. Do you understand this?'

'Now that Gorgiano is dead we are afraid of nothing,' said Mrs Lucca. 'He was a terrible monster. But I know Gennaro did the wrong thing; killing is always wrong.' She was silent for a moment and her dark eyes were sad.

'If I tell you the whole story, perhaps you will understand why my husband killed him.'

'Very well,' said Holmes, 'let's close this door and leave everything here. We can go with this lady to her room and listen to her story.'

We all went back to Mrs Warren's house. Half an hour later we were sitting in Mrs Lucca's small sitting-room. She started telling us her unusual story. She spoke very quickly but her English was not good.

'I was born in Posilippo, near the city of Naples, Italy,' she said. 'I am the daughter of Augusto Barelli, a very important man. Gennaro worked for my father and I loved him. He was poor, but he was handsome and kind. My father did not let me marry him, so we ran away together. We got married in another city. Then I sold my jewels [2] to get the money to go to America. We went to New York City four years ago and stayed there. There were a lot of Italians in New York and we liked it.

'At first everything went well. Gennaro helped an Italian gentleman called Tito Castalotte, and became his good friend. Mr Castalotte owns a big company in New York and more than three hundred men work for him. He gave Gennaro an important job in his company and

2. jewels :

was always kind to him. Mr Castalotte was not married and Gennaro was like a son to him. We both loved him like a father. Gennaro and I rented a small house in Brooklyn [3] and we were happy together.

'Then one evening Gennaro brought an Italian man home with him. His name was Giuseppe Gorgiano and he was from Posilippo too. He was so big, as you know. Everything about him was big and frightening. His voice was loud and he moved his enormous arms about when he talked. He was too big for our little house. He never stopped talking with his loud, angry voice. He came to our house again and again. Gennaro was unhappy when Gorgiano was at our house. But he sat and listened to Gorgiano talk. He was a very bad man and he was always angry.'

We were all listening carefully to Mrs Lucca's long story.

'I knew something was wrong. My poor Gennaro was terribly afraid of him. One night Gennaro told me his long story and I became very sad. When Gennaro was young he was poor, and the world was against him. He became a member of a secret society in Naples called the Red Circle. It was part of the old Carbonari [4] and it did terrible things. The members of this secret society had to follow the rules and could not leave it.

'When we went to America Gennaro was happy because he was far from Naples and the Red Circle. He wanted to forget about it. But one evening he met a member of the Red Circle in New York – it was Giuseppe Gorgiano. In the South of Italy people called him "Death" because he was a terrible killer. He went to New York because the Italian police wanted to arrest him. And in his new city he started the Red Circle again.'

---

3. **Brooklyn** : an area of New York City.
4. **Carbonari** : a secret Italian society of the early 1800s.

UNDERSTANDING THE TEXT

1 COMPREHENSION CHECK

Read the paragraphs and choose the best word (A, B or C) for each space. There is an example at the beginning (0).

The beautiful young woman was (**0**)...C... Emilia Lucca. She was Gennaro Lucca's wife. When she saw Gorgiano's body (**1**)....... the floor she was very surprised. She said that Gennaro was probably the killer. Holmes asked Emilia to tell (**2**)....... story to everyone.

Emilia was born (**3**)....... Posilippo, Italy. She loved Gennaro but her father did not want her to marry (**4**)....... . They decided to run away together and (**5**)....... married. Then they went to New York. Gennaro (**6**)....... a good job and made friends with Tito Castalotte.

One evening Gennaro brought home (**7**)....... Italian man called Giuseppe Gorgiano. He was big and frightening, and his voice was very loud. Emilia did not like him.

When Gennaro was young and poor he (**8**)....... a member of a secret society called the Red Circle. This secret society did terrible things and its members could not leave it. In America Gennaro wanted to (**9**)....... about the Red Circle. But he (**10**)....... one of its members in New York: Gorgiano.

0	**A** name	**B** call	**C** called
1	**A** to	**B** aat	**C** on
2	**A** them	**B** her	**C** she
3	**A** in	**B** to	**C** at
4	**A** him	**B** he	**C** it
5	**A** be	**B** get	**C** have
6	**A** found	**B** find	**C** finding
7	**A** an	**B** a	**C** the
8	**A** become	**B** becoming	**C** became
9	**A** forget	**B** forgot	**C** forgetting
10	**A** meet	**B** met	**C** meeting

2 CHARACTERS

Use words from the box to describe the characters below.

dark eyes   huge   tall   frightening   handsome   young
loud voice   beautiful   angry   bad   dark hair   big arms   kind

EMILIA
....
....
....

GORGIANO
....
....
....

GENNARO
....
....
....

KET

3 WRITING

**Read this postcard from Emilia's best friend in Brooklyn. Then write
Sally a postcard from Emilia. Answer her questions. Write 25-35 words.**

This Space for Writing Messages

P**OST**C**ARD**

Dear Emilia,
It's cold here in Brooklyn
and it's snowing.
How about London? Is it
cold? What's the weather
like? Are you and Gennaro
happy there? Where are you
staying?
Please send me a postcard.

Love, Sally

THE GREAT EAST RIVER SUSPENSION BRIDGE,

Dear Sally,
....
....
....
....
....

4 A COUNTRY OF IMMIGRANTS

Emilia and Gennaro moved from Italy to America, like a lot of other Europeans at that time. Read the information below about nineteenth-century America and its immigrants and fill in the gaps with the correct past simple form of the verb in brackets.

Between 1820 and 1919 about 50 million people from European countries such as Germany, Ireland, France, the Netherlands, Sweden, Italy, Austria, Hungary, Russia and Great Britain (**1**) .... (*emigrate*) to the United States. They wanted a better life for themselves and their children. Some immigrants (**2**) .... (*have*) political and religious problems in their own country and (**3**) .... (*go*) to America to find freedom.

The first immigrants (**4**) .... (*arrive*) in the 1840s when there was a terrible food problems in northern Europe, particularly in Ireland.

At that time America was a very big country with very few people. It had a lot of natural resources and there were jobs and great economic opportunities for everyone. The American government often (**5**) .... (*give*) land to people who wanted to live there.

In 1848 John Marshall (**6**) .... (*discover*) gold at Sutter's Fort in California, on the West coast of America. This started the 'California Gold Rush'. People from all over the world (**7**) .... (*travel*) to California to look for gold and a lot of them stayed there after the Gold Rush.

The transcontinental railway across the United States was completed in 1869 and it (**8**) .... (*bring*) hundreds of thousands of immigrants to the West coast.

Between 1890 and 1924 most immigrants came from Italy, Greece and the Balkan countries.

During the nineteenth century about three quarters of the immigrants went to New York City because there (**9**) .... (*be*) a lot of work in the new industries and businesses. In the year 1800 the population of New York City was 60,000; in the late 1800s it (**10**) .... (*grow*) to 800,000! It became one of America's biggest and most important cities.

BEFORE YOU READ

 1 LISTENING

Listen to the first part of Chapter Seven and choose the correct answer – A, B or C.

1 What did Gorgiano's letter say?
- **A** ☐ The Red Circle wanted money from Gennaro.
- **B** ☐ Gennaro had to go to a meeting.
- **C** ☐ Gennaro and Emilia had to go to an important dinner.

2 What was Gorgiano's secret?
- **A** ☐ He wanted to kill Gennaro.
- **B** ☐ He was Gennaro's brother.
- **C** ☐ He loved Emilia.

3 What happened when Gennaro came home?
- **A** ☐ He fought with Gorgiano.
- **B** ☐ He ran away because he was afraid of Gorgiano.
- **C** ☐ He kissed Emilia.

4 Who went to talk to the New York police?
- **A** ☐ Gennaro
- **B** ☐ Tito Castalotte
- **C** ☐ Gorgiano

5 What did the Red Circle tell Gennaro to do?
- **A** ☐ send Castalotte a letter.
- **B** ☐ get money from Castalotte.
- **C** ☐ blow up Castalotte's house.

6 What did Gennaro and Emilia decide to do?
- **A** ☐ go to the police
- **B** ☐ leave New York
- **C** ☐ return to Italy

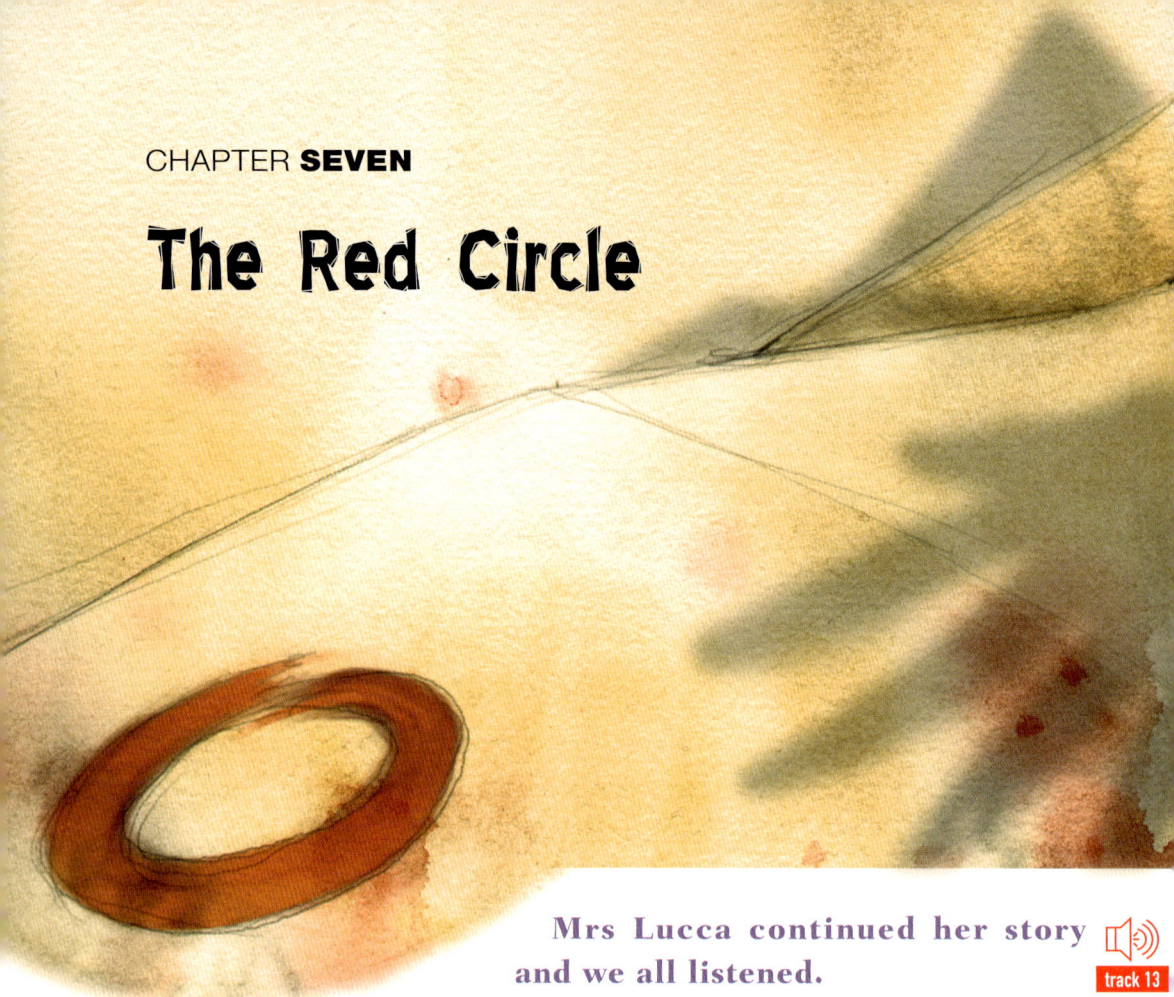

CHAPTER SEVEN

The Red Circle

Mrs Lucca continued her story and we all listened.

track 13

'One evening Gennaro showed me a letter from Gorgiano with a red circle at the top. It said there was an important meeting on a certain day and Gennaro had to go. This was terrible, but then something worse happened.

'Gorgiano always came to see us in the evening. He talked to me a lot and I did not like it. He always looked at me with his big ugly eyes. I did not know what to do. Then one night Gorgiano came to our house when I was alone. Gennaro was still at work and Gorgiano told me his secret: he loved me! He took me in his huge arms and kissed me. It was terrible and I screamed. [1]

At that moment Gennaro came home and tried to help me. He and Gorgiano fought a lot, and Gorgiano knocked him down and

---

1. **screamed** : made a loud sound because I was very frightened.

ran away. He never came back to our house. Gorgiano became our dangerous enemy.'

Mrs Lucca stopped for a moment and looked at us with sad eyes. Then she continued.

'A few days later there was the meeting of the Red Circle and Gennaro had to go. When he came back his face was white. To get money the secret society blackmailed [2] rich Italians who lived in New York. The Red Circle did terrible things to the Italians who did not pay. It even killed them!

'The Red Circle sent a letter to our friend Tito Castalotte and told him to pay. He was frightened and angry and told the New York police about Gorgiano and the Red Circle. Gorgiano was very angry and decided to blow up [3] Castalotte's house. The members of the Red Circle chose Gennaro to do it. He had to kill his best friend!

'My poor Gennaro was terrified. He is a good man, he is not a killer. He looked at me and said, "If I don't kill Castalotte, Gorgiano will kill us!"

'It was a terrible night. Gennaro and I were very, very afraid. We could not sleep and we did not know what to do. We talked all night about Gorgiano, the Red Circle, Castalotte and all of the problems we had. Finally we decided it was too dangerous to stay in New York and we had to leave immediately. But where could we go? I wanted to go back to Posilippo, but Gennaro said that it was not possible. There were too many of Gorgiano's friends and other Red Circle members there. So we decided to leave for London because it is a big city and we know no one. We left early

2. **blackmailed** : forced them to pay money.

3. **blow up** :

the next morning, before the sun came up. We didn't bring anything with us, only clothes and documents because we didn't want anyone to realise we were leaving. We went to the port, but before, we sent messages to both Castalotte and the police to tell them about Gorgiano's terrible plan.

'Well, gentlemen, you already know the rest of the story. Gorgiano followed us to London and Gennaro found a place for me to hide. He wanted to go and talk to the Italian police. I never saw my husband during this time. I don't know where he lived or what he did. The only news from Gennaro were the messages in the newspaper. Then one day from the window I saw two Italians in the street; it was Gorgiano and another man. They were watching the house. I was alone and frightened.

'I read Gennaro's messages in the newspaper. I waited at the window for his signals and saw them. I knew there was great danger because Gorgiano was near. Fortunately Gennaro was ready for him when he came. Now, gentlemen, you know the whole story – a long and sad one.'

'Well, Mr Gregson,' said the American detective, 'Now we know the whole story. What do you think?'

'Gennaro Lucca killed a man. Mrs Lucca has to come with me to Scotland Yard,' said Gregson. 'The Chief of Police has to hear her story and talk to her husband. Then he'll decide what to do.'

'Well, Watson,' said Holmes, 'I think our work is done and it's time to go.' He turned to Emilia and to the other men and said, 'Good evening everyone.'

Holmes and I got up, put on our coats and left. It was a cold night as we walked out of Mrs Warren's house.

UNDERSTANDING THE TEXT

1 COMPREHENSION CHECK
Match the following sentences (1–9) with their endings (A–I).

1 ☐ Gennaro received a letter
2 ☐ Gennaro and Gorgiano fought a lot
3 ☐ The Red Circle blackmailed rich Italians
4 ☐ Tito Castalotte did not want to pay the Red Circle
5 ☐ Gorgiano wanted to blow up Castalotte's house
6 ☐ Gennaro was terrified, and he and Emilia decided
7 ☐ In London Gennaro hid Emilia
8 ☐ In the end Gennaro
9 ☐ The four men listened to Emilia's story and

A and went to the New York police.
B to go to London.
C to get money from them.
D with a red circle on top of it.
E at Mrs Warren's house.
F and Gennaro had to do it.
G and Gorgiano knocked Gennaro down and ran away.
H killed Gorgiano.
I Gregson asked her to go to Scotland Yard with him.

T: GRADE 3

2 SPEAKING: THE WEATHER
It is a foggy evening when Holmes and Watson leave Mrs Warren's house. Talk to your partner about the weather. Use these questions to help you.

- What's the weather like where you live?
- What is your favourite kind of weather and why?
- What is winter like in your area?
- Do you play winter sports?
- What do you do when the weather is very hot?

3 VOCABULARY – NATIONALITIES

A Sherlock Holmes, Mr Leverton and Emilia Lucca come from Great Britain, the United States and Italy. Do you know how to say their nationalities? Work with a partner and fill in the table below. You can use a dictionary to help you.

Great Britain...............................	Poland ....
The United States of America	Switzerland ....
Italy...	Ireland..
Spain	Japan..
Russia..	Greece ....
China	Portugal ....
Germany	Mexico..
France	Australia......................................
The Netherlands.........................	Canada ....
Turkey	Denmark ....

B Now complete the sentences using some of the nationalities.

1 Emilia and Gennaro are ....
2 Pinkerton's is a famous .... detective agency.
3 She comes from the Netherlands; she's ....
4 They spent the summer in Greece and learned to speak
  ....
5 The .... government invited Sherlock Holmes to Turkey to solve a case.
6 The group U2 are ....

Complete this crossword puzzle.

Across

2

3 The opposite of full.

7

8 To force someone to pay money.

11 This person rents a room in someone's house.

12 An American detective agency.

14

15 A park in London, Hampstead ....

16 The country where Emilia and Gennaro come from.

Down

1

2 An area of New York City.

4

5

6 A document the police use when they arrest someone.

9 To make a loud sound when you are frightened of something.

10 You use this to wash.

13

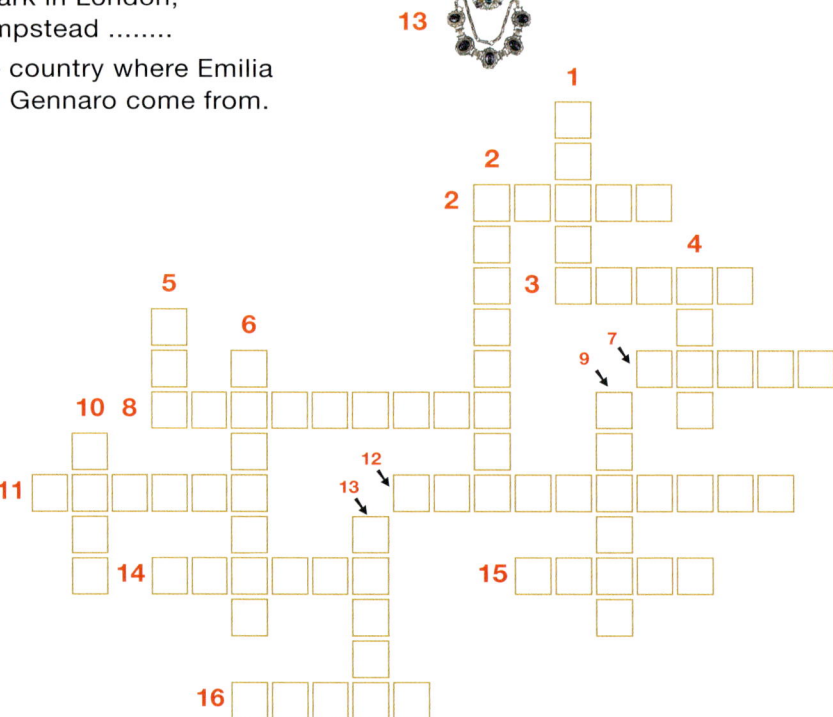

AFTER READING

Are the following sentences true (T) or false (F)? Correct the false ones.

		T	F
1	Sherlock Holmes decided to help Mrs Warren because she gave him ten pounds.	☐	☐
2	Mrs Warren was frightened because she never saw the lodger but heard his footsteps at night.	☐	☐
3	The lodger read the *Daily Gazette*.	☐	☐
4	Mr Warren went to the police because two men pushed him into a cab one morning.	☐	☐
5	Holmes and Watson saw the lodger's face in the mirror.	☐	☐
6	Holmes thought the lodger was a dangerous criminal.	☐	☐
7	Gorgiano sent messages to the lodger using the flame of the candle.	☐	☐
8	Holmes and Watson met Gregson and Leverton outside the red building.	☐	☐
9	Leverton came from New York because he wanted to arrest Gennaro Lucca.	☐	☐
10	Gorgiano's body was on the floor in Mrs Warren's house.	☐	☐
11	Emilia and Gennaro met Tito Castalotte in New York and became good friends.	☐	☐
12	The Red Circle told Gennaro to kill Tito Castalotte.	☐	☐
13	Emilia and Gennaro went to London to meet Gorgiano.	☐	☐
14	Gregson asked Emilia to go with him to Scotland Yard.	☐	☐

2 PICTURE SUMMARY

Look at the pictures from *Sherlock Holmes and the Red Circle* below. They are not in the right order. Put them in the order in which they appear in the story.

  A

 B

....

....

 C

 D

....

....

This reader uses the **EXPANSIVE READING** approach, where the text becomes a springboard to improve language skills and to explore historical background, cultural connections and other topics suggested by the text.

The new structures introduced in this step of our **GREEN APPLE** series are listed below. Naturally, structures from lower steps are included too. For a complete list of structures used over all the three steps, see *The Black Cat Guide to Graded Readers*, which is also downloadable at no cost from our website, blackcat-cideb.com.

The vocabulary used at each step is carefully checked against vocabulary lists used for internationally recognised examinations.

Step 1 A2

All the structures used in the previous step, plus the following:

Verb tenses
Past Simple
Past Continuous
Future reference: *will*

Verb forms and patterns
Regular and common irregular verbs
Passive forms: Present Simple and Past Simple with very
  common verbs (e.g. *made, called, born*)
Gerunds (verb + *-ing*) after some prepositions
  (e.g. *before, after*)

Modal verbs
Could: ability; requests
Will: future reference; offers; promises; predictions
May (present and future reference): possibility
Mustn't: prohibition
Have (got) to: external obligation

Types of clause
Subordination after *if* (zero and 1st conditionals)
Defining relative clauses with: *who, where*

Other
Comparative and superlative of adjectives
  (regular and irregular)
Formation of adverbs (regular and irregular)

E

....
....

F

....
....

G

H

....
....

3 **A GRAPHIC NOVEL**

Photocopy these two pages, cut out the pictures and stick them on
paper in the right order. Think of words to put in speech or thought
bubbles to show what the characters are saying or thinking. Do not
use the words that were used in this book! In small groups retell the
story.